PROPERTY OF
FREDERICKSBURG CITY SCHOOLS

a cat is

a cat is

by Adrien Stoutenburg

photographs by Sy Katzoff

Franklin Watts, Inc.
845 Third Avenue | New York, N.Y. 10022

10 9 8 7 6 5 4 3 2

SBN 531-01969-1
Text Copyright © 1971 by Adrien Stoutenburg
Photographs Copyright © 1971 by Seymour Katzoff

Library of Congress Catalog Card Number: 77-134658
Printed in the United States of America

17659

To that feline mistress
of the Lebman household,
Colette

A cat is
    very nice to meet
    anywhere.

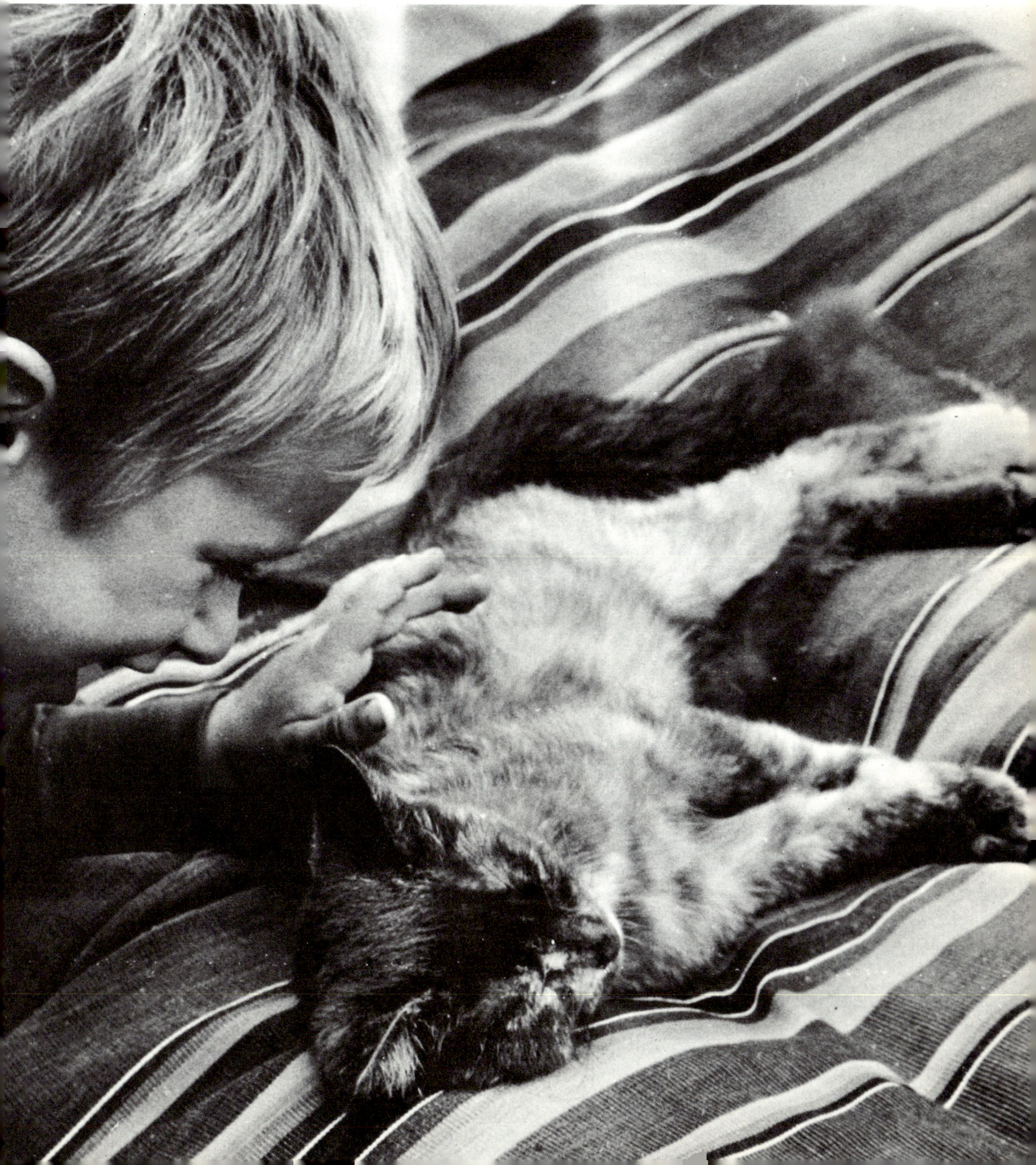

He walks on feet
so soft,

you hardly know he's there
beside a tree
or on a stair

or chasing shadows
through the sun
and down the street—
or catching them
beneath your chair.

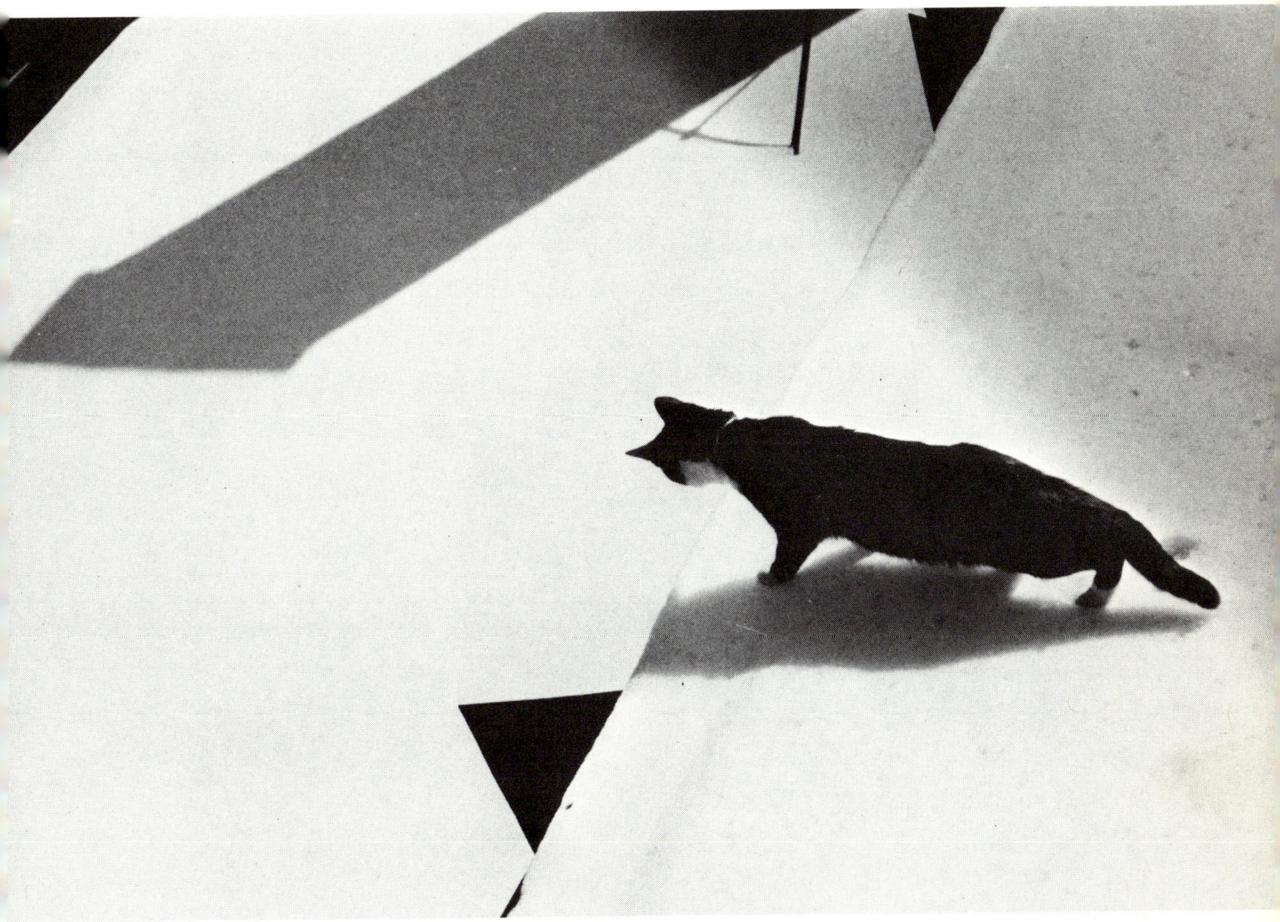

A cat is
> always a kitten first,
> which is mostly fluff
> with a tail fastened on.
> And four round legs
> just long enough
> to keep him up
> instead of down.

A kitten is quiet
and full of sleep

except when he's awake
and mewing,
and climbing where
he shouldn't climb,
and doing things
he shouldn't be doing—

But kittens must do
the things they want to
if they want to be kittens
and grow into cats,
which, of course, they do.

Wouldn't you?

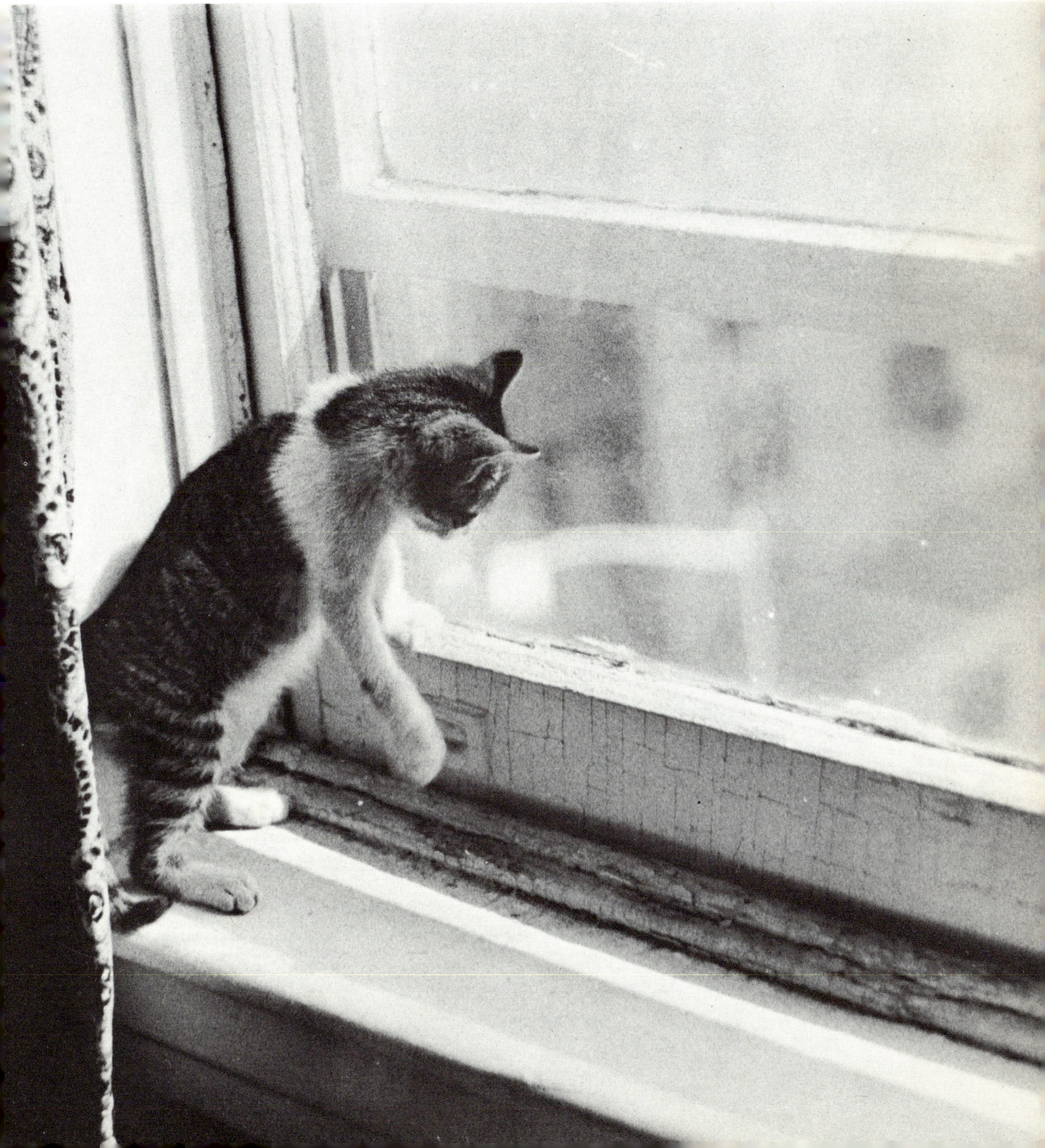

A cat is
>   soft and warm, and sings,
>   and likes to play with twisty things
>   like yarn and strings
>   or bouncy balls.
>   He also thinks bare toes are nice,
>   especially if they move like mice.

It's safer, when he wants to play,
to keep your shoes on
(at least partway),
and offer him some other toy
instead of you.
A leaf, or just a shadow,
will do.

A cat is
    proud and does as he wishes.
    He won't learn tricks
    and he won't do dishes;
    he won't eat his food
    if it's cold or too hot;
    he won't sit still
    if he'd rather not.

He may let you scratch
his ears and chin,
or let him out
and let him in.
And he may, if he's sleepy,
climb into your lap
and hum a little
before a long nap—
unless you *try*
to get him there.
Don't!
If you do,
he won't.

A cat is
>polite and very neat.
>He purrs a "thank you"
>when you give him a treat.

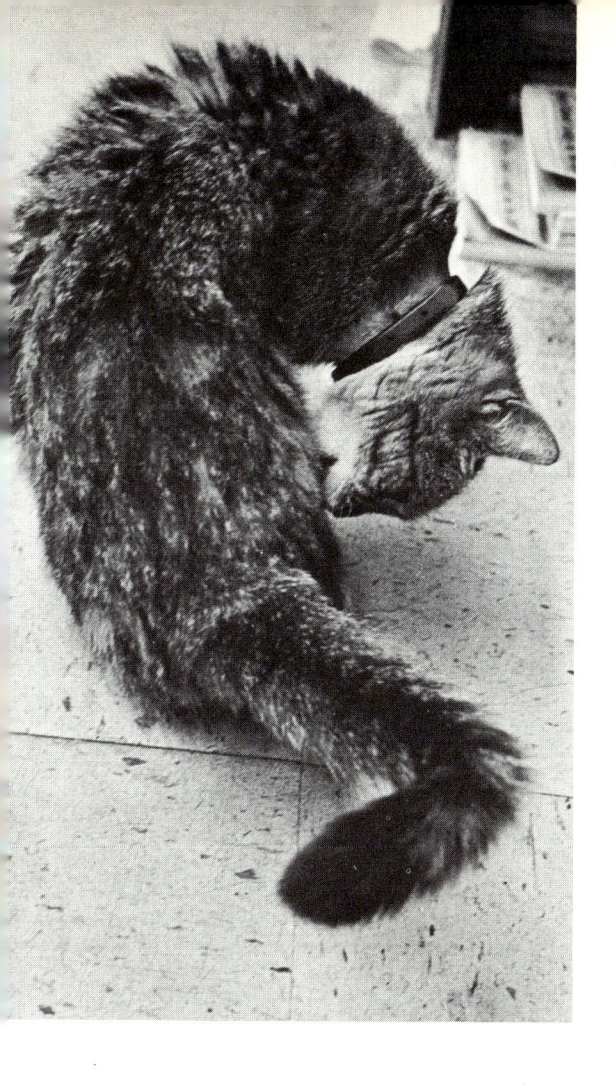

And after he's through,
he washes his face
and his two bright ears
and his four pink feet,
his one short nose
and his one long tail.
And everything else
that he can reach,
which is quite a bit,
since a cat can bend,
easily,
from end to end.

A cat is
>cuddly except for his claws,
>but he keeps them tucked
>within his paws,
>unless you tease him
>or get in the way
>when he thinks he's hunting
>some larger prey.

He cleans his claws
on a tree, if he has one.
If he doesn't, a sofa
or a rug will do—
which is bad for the rug
and sad for the sofa,
but better than his making
a tree out of you.

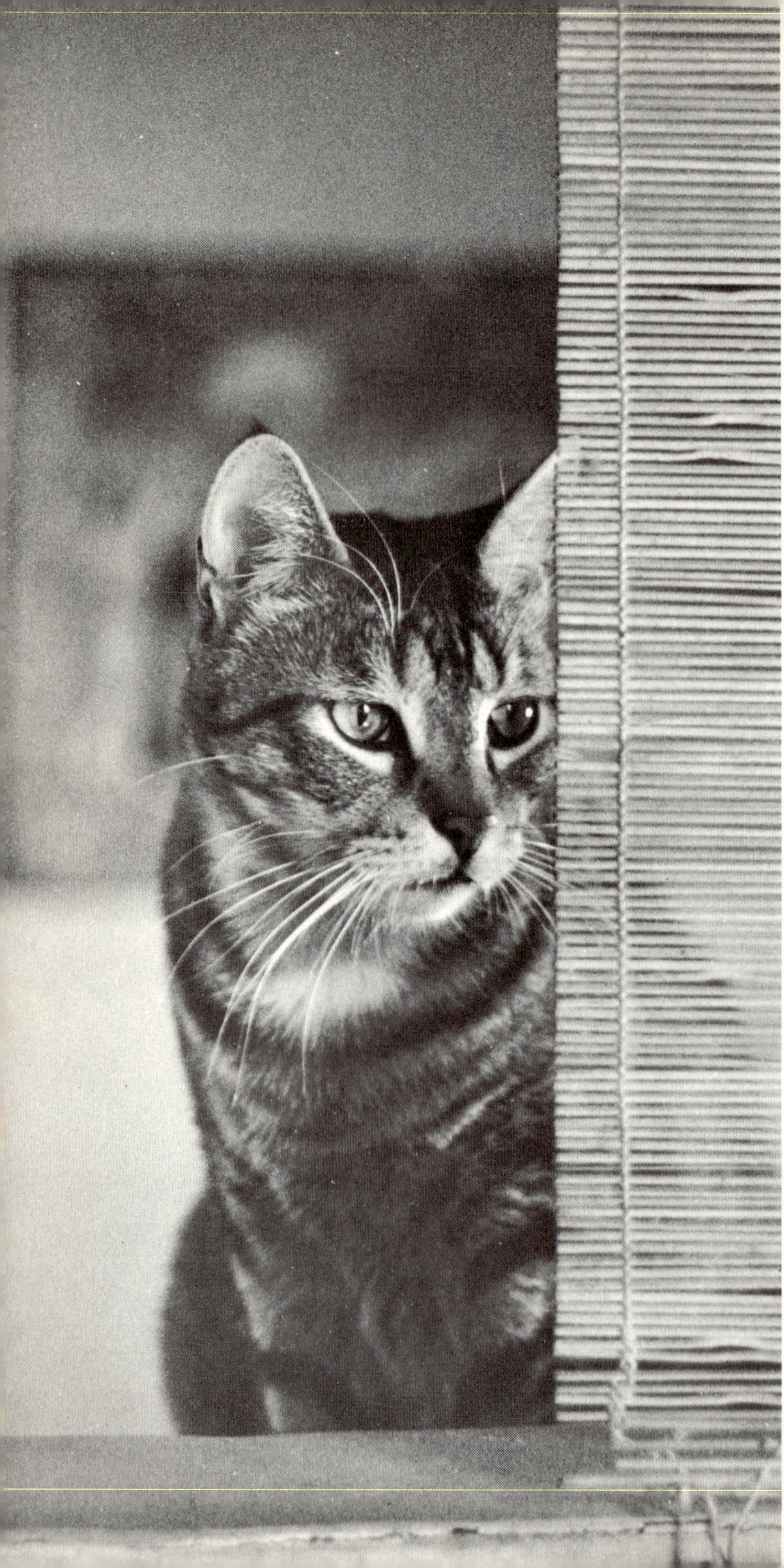

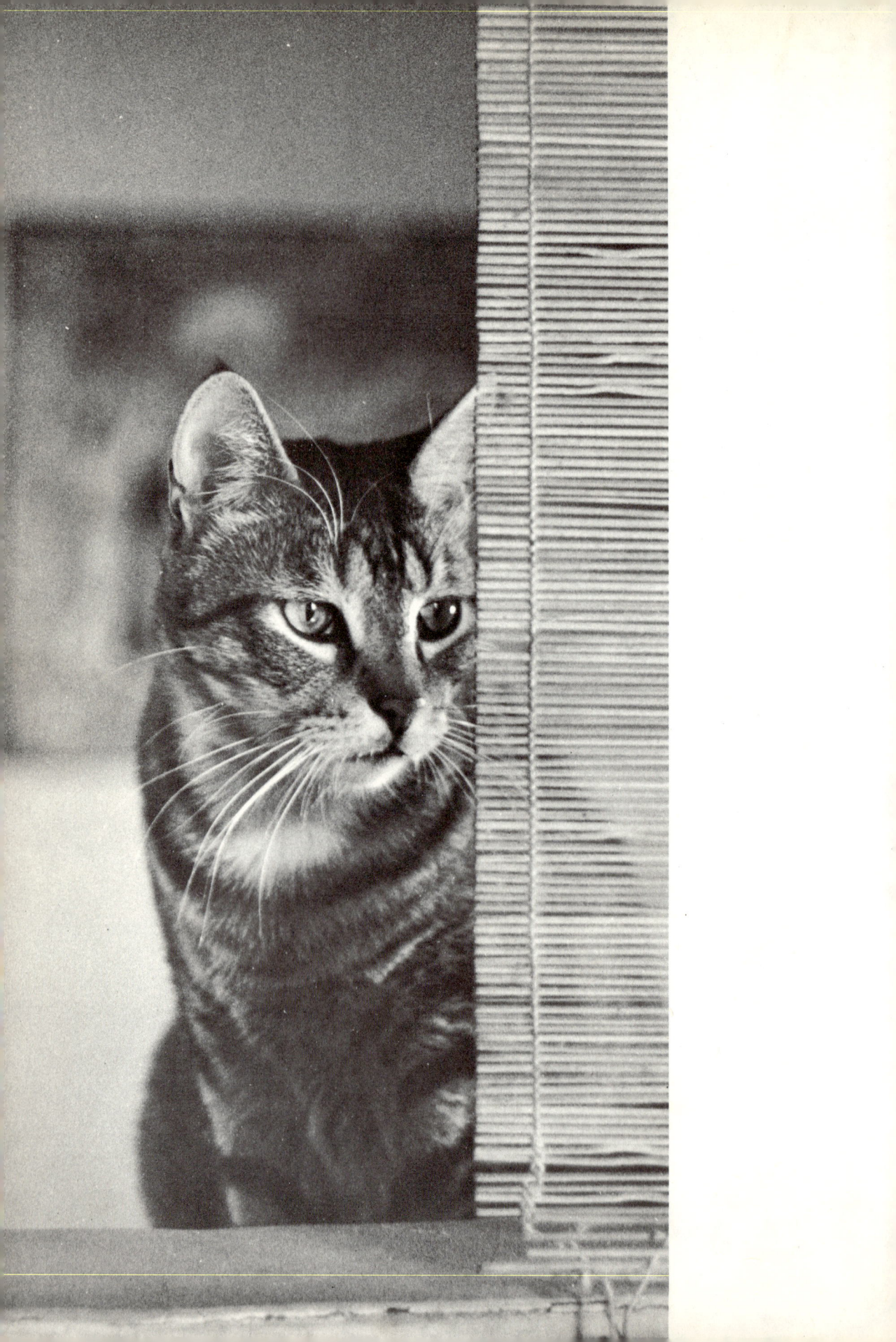

A cat is
  a watcher
  of many things.
  He watches for mice,
  he watches for wings,
  and he watches the rain.

If you'll give him a window
that looks at the sky,
he'll sit there for hours
(though you don't know why).

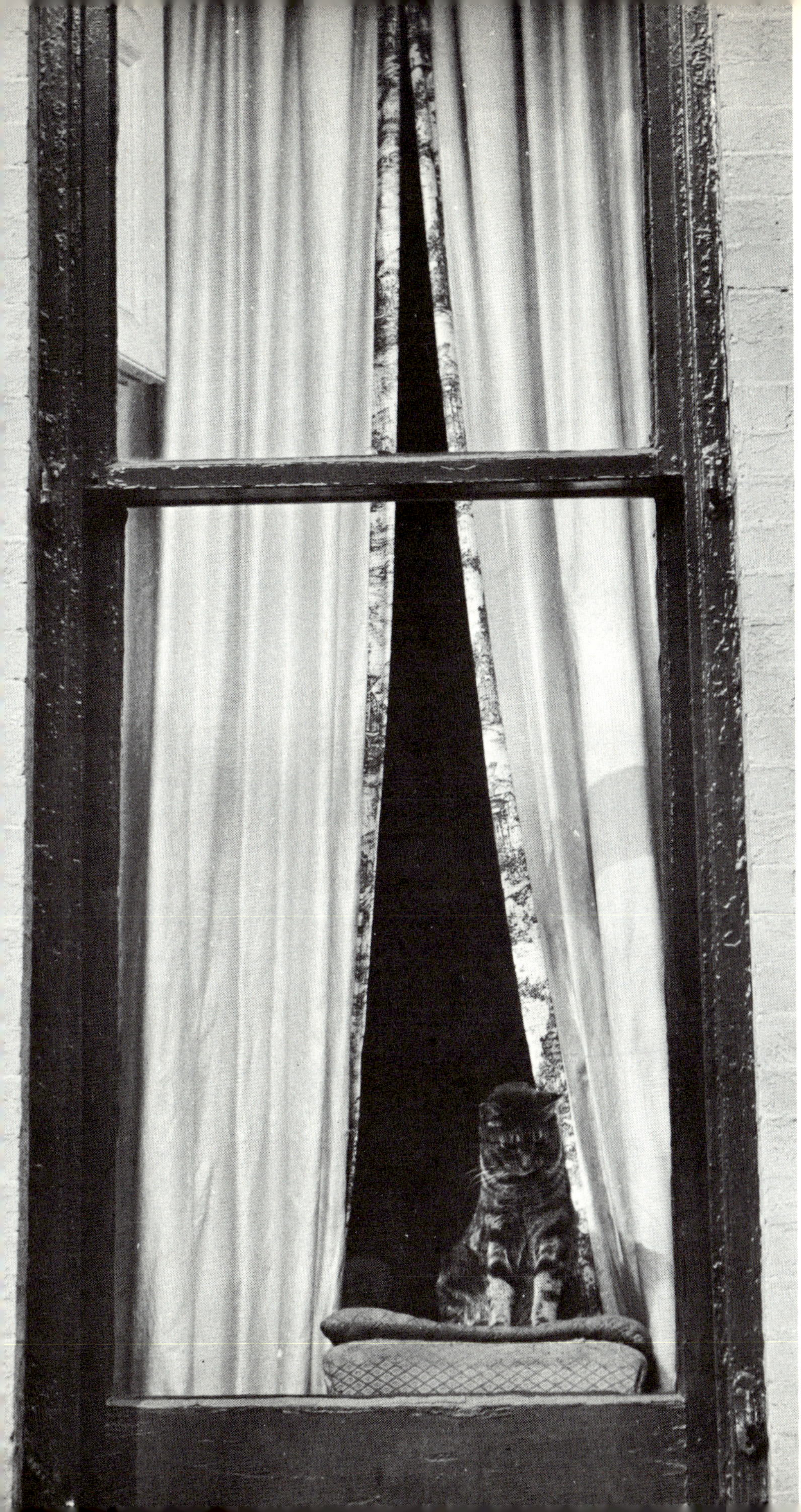

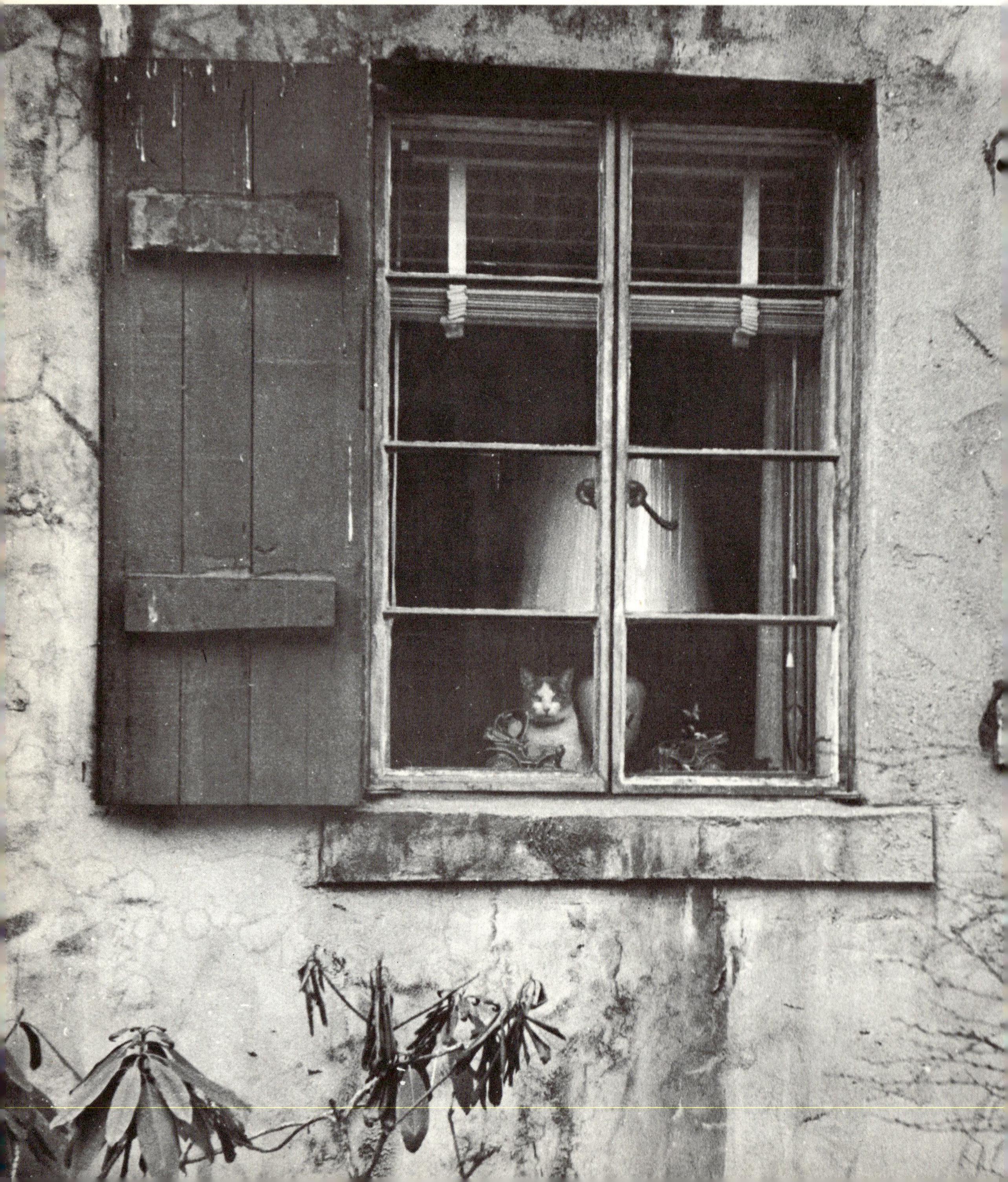

He must see something
we don't always see.
It could be a cricket,

it could be a tree
with one moving leaf,
or only the tip
of a tiny bud opening,
or a great bumblebee.

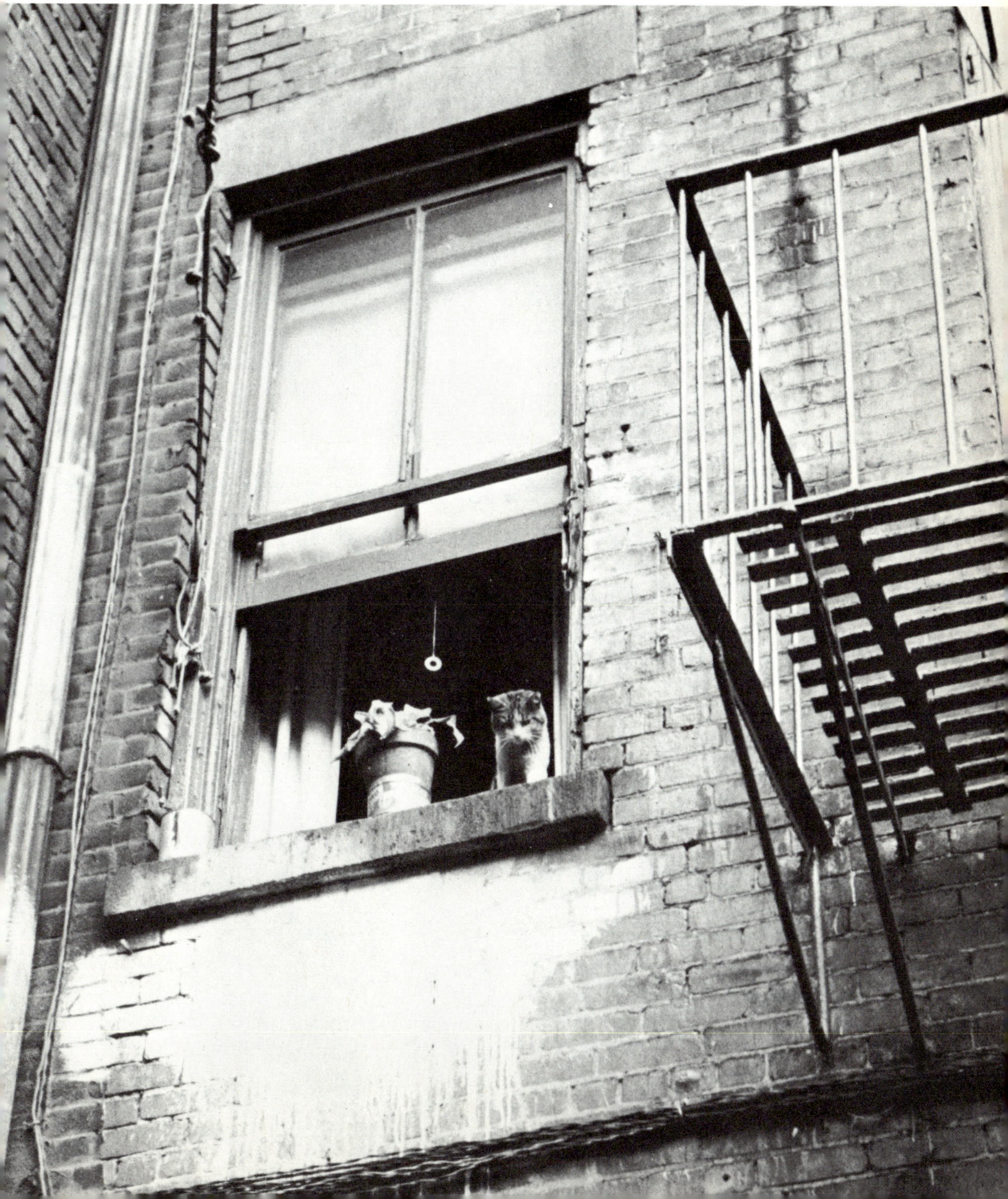

The strange thing is,
sometimes he seems to stare
with both his eyes shut,
at whatever is there.

If you want to begin
to know what he's about,
the only thing to think
is
that he's looking in,
not out.

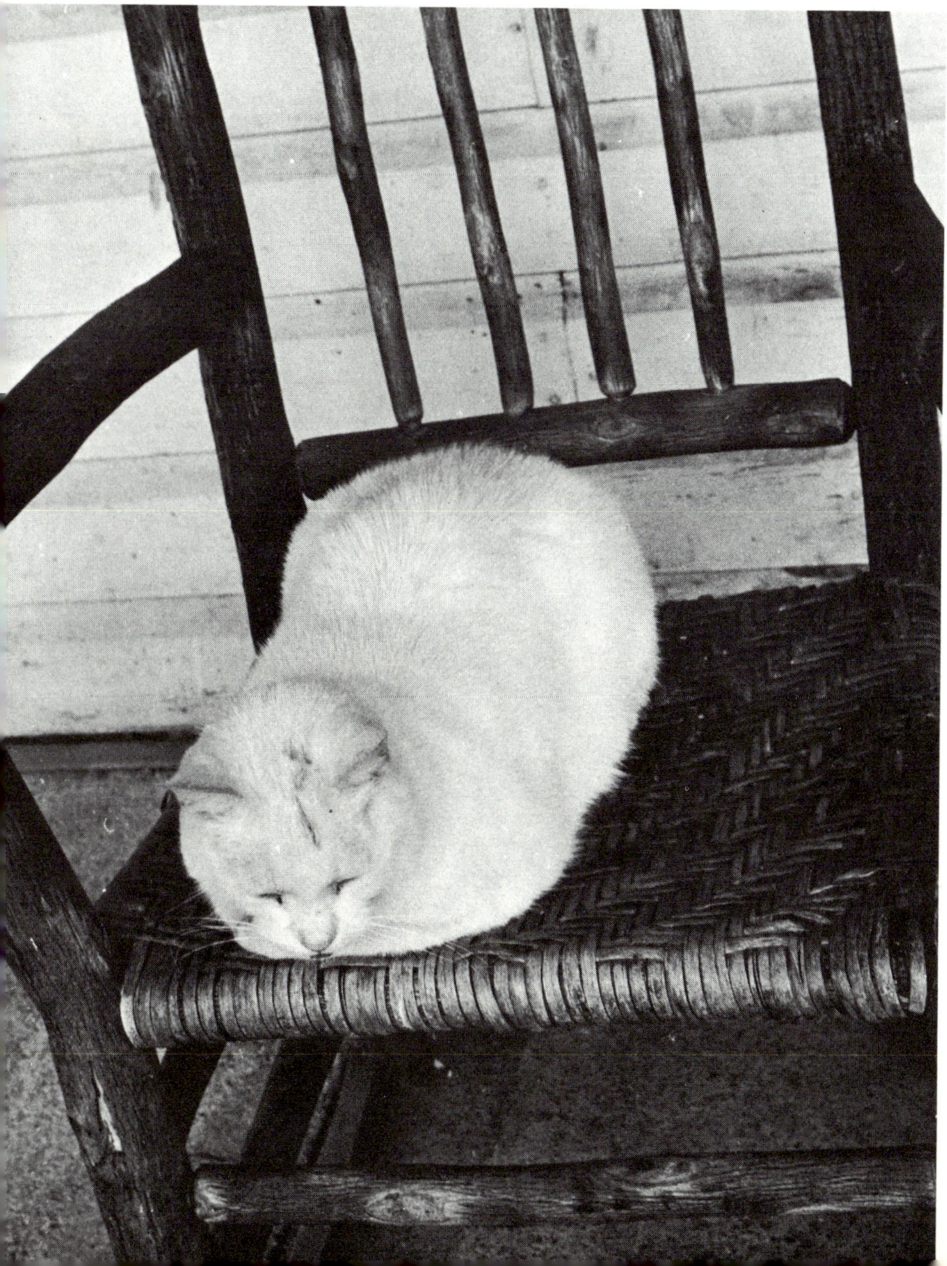

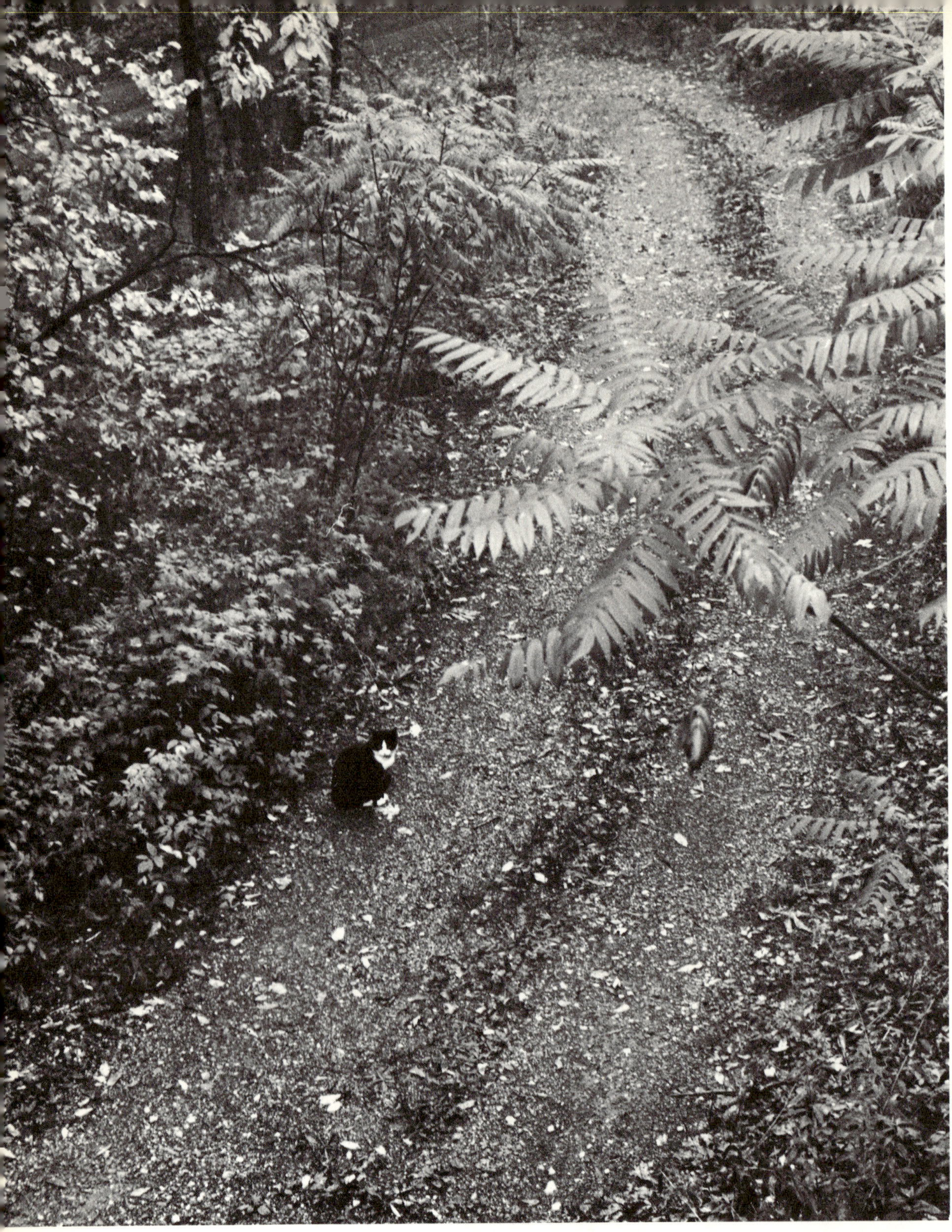

A cat is
>   free,
>   or wants to be.
>   He doesn't like cages,
>   or boxes or doors
>   that are closed too long—
>   and what he abhors
>   is a rope on his neck.

But he likes very much
a rattly hutch
like a paper bag,
which he can pretend
is a terrible, horrible,
unbearable cage.

He can tear that to shreds
and tatters and threads;
he can break it and rake it
and shake it to death,
then walk away
with his tail in the air,
as if to say, "There!
You can't trap me.
For a cat must be free,
as I'm going to be."

And, of course,
we know one thing is true:
you can't own a cat;
it's the cat who owns you.

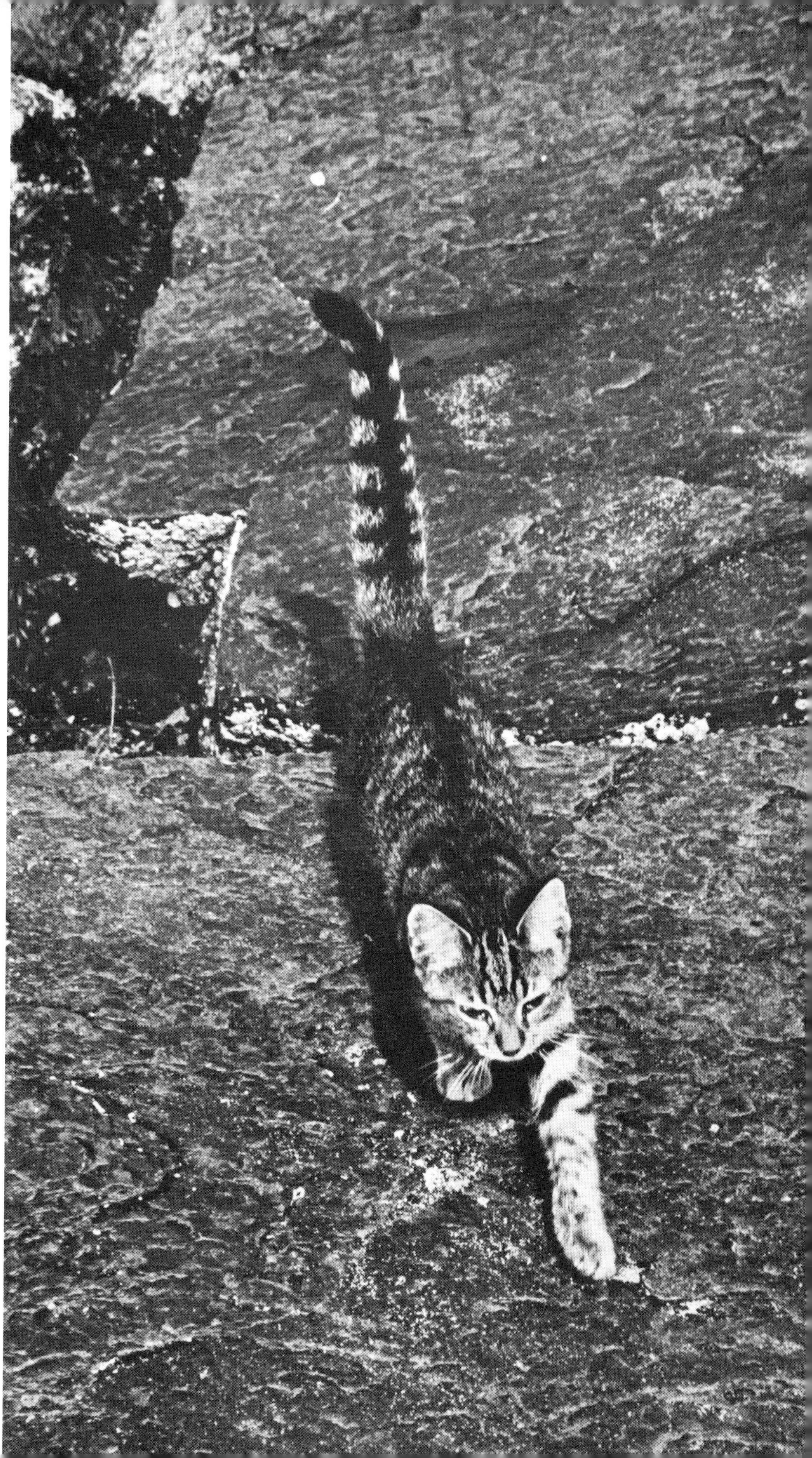

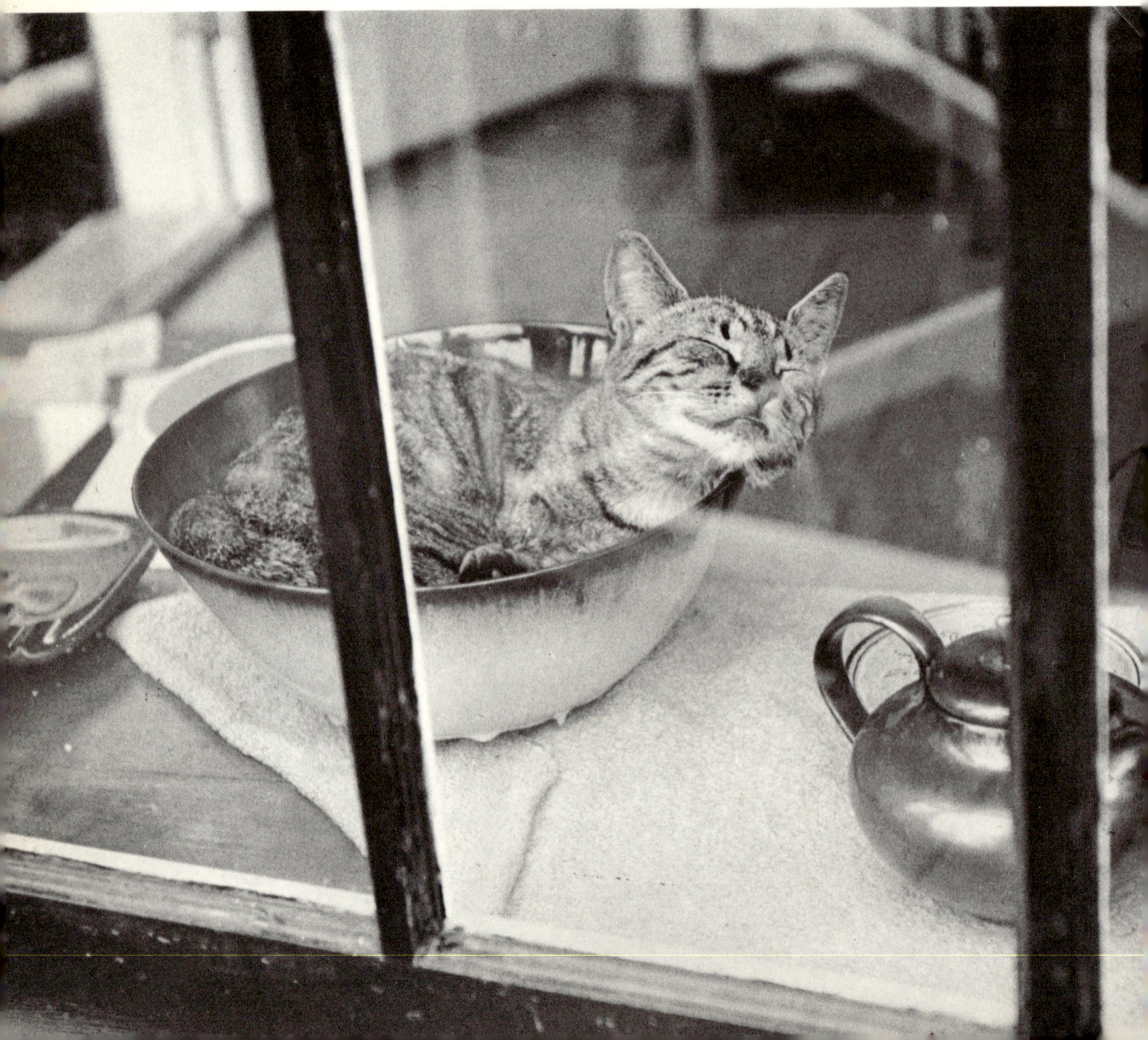

A cat is
    not somebody
    you can shake hands with
    or hug.
    But if you want to be snug,
    with your hands warm on fur,
    or just watch something
    that can leap like light
    or that can be as still
    as wind in a jar,
    you needn't look far.

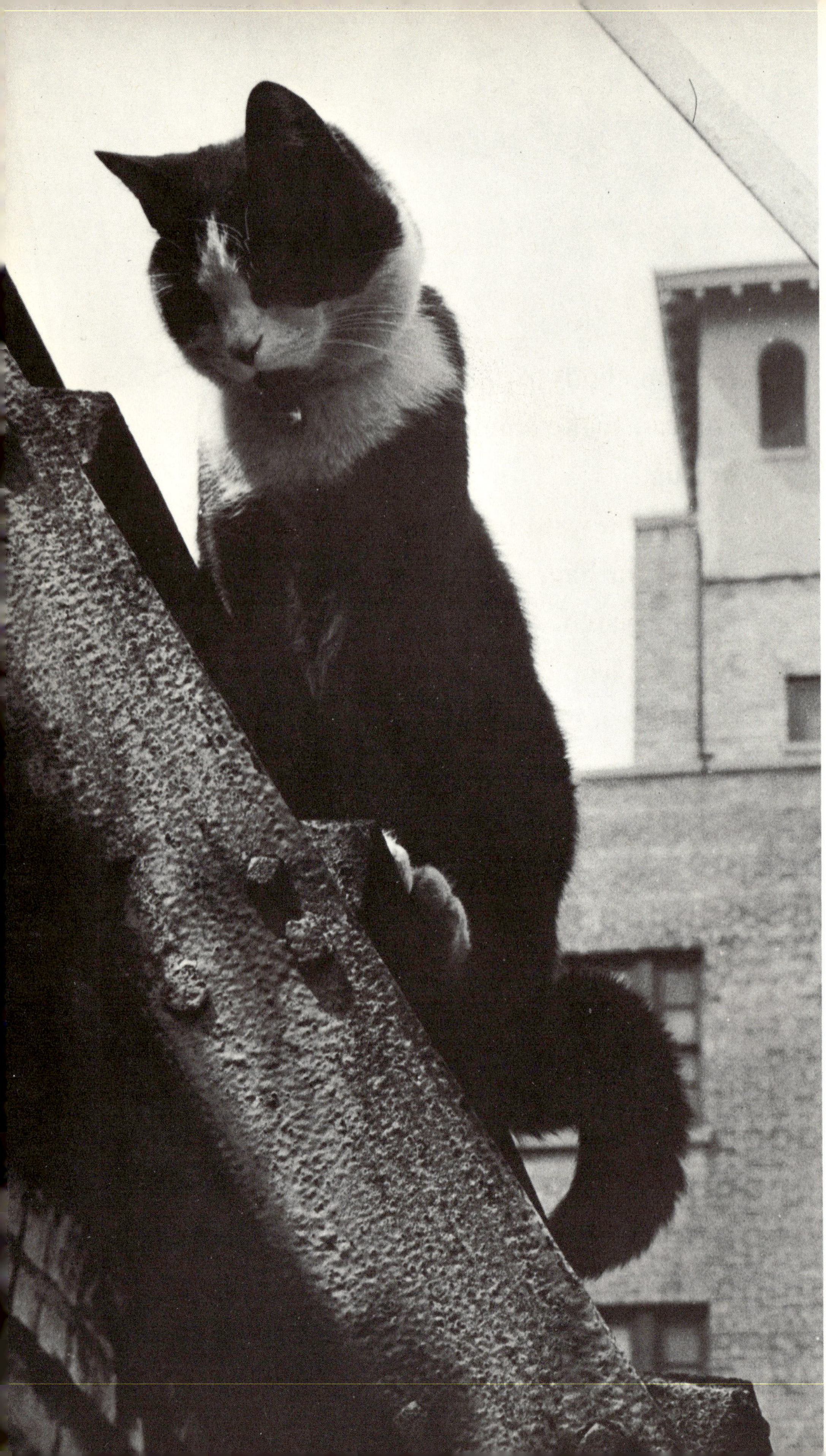

A cat is that,
and more.
And cats are everywhere:
up on a roof,
hunting in a shed,
hiding in a basket—
or in your bed.

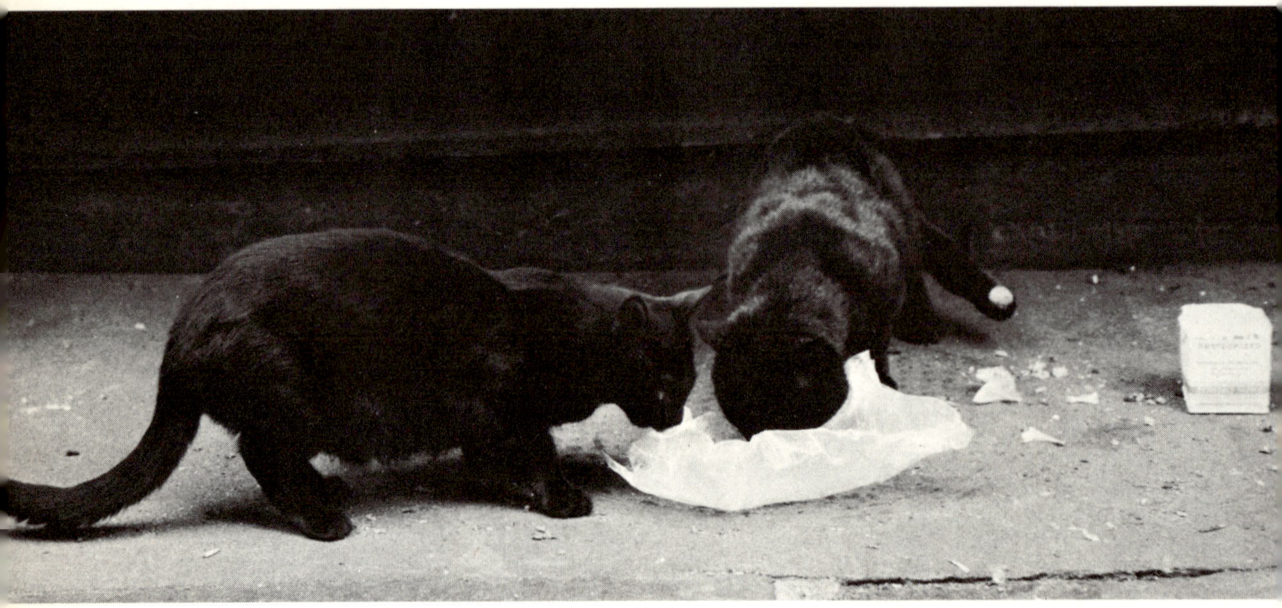

Whatever a cat is
and whatever he's doing,
playing or eating
or just plain mewing,
and whether he's gray
or yellow or black
or even pink
(though I've never seen that),
or long or short,
bony or fat

A cat is

forever and always

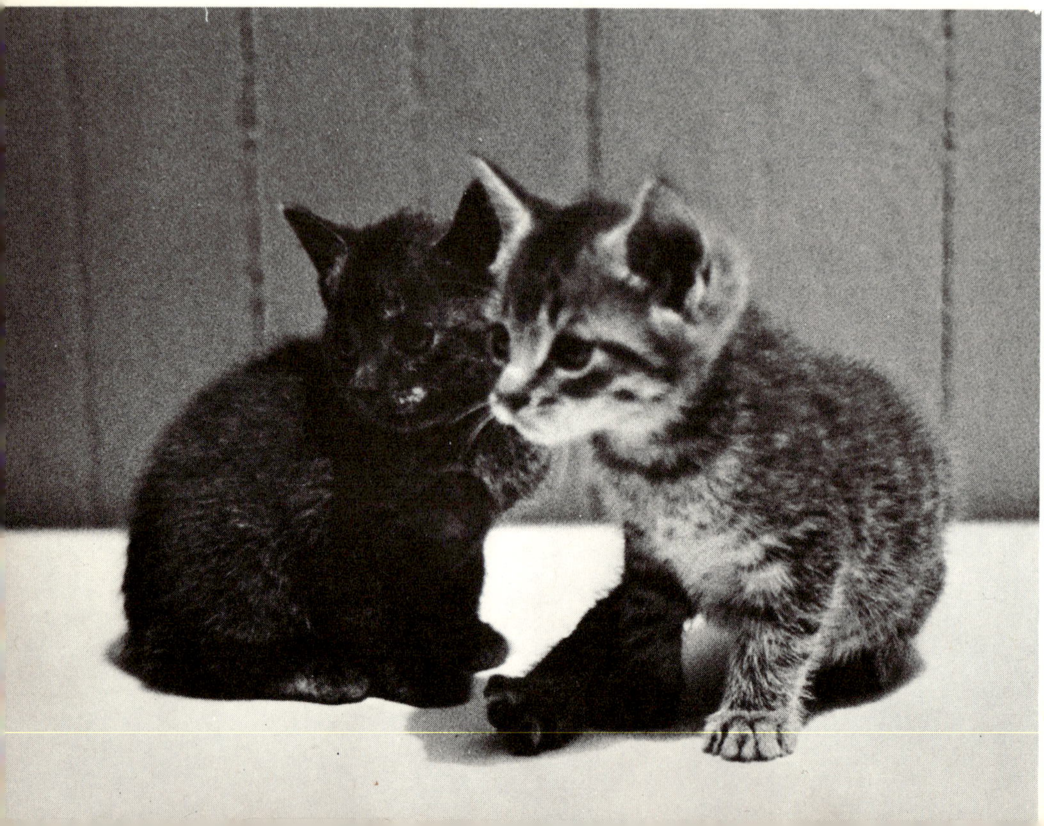

A CAT.

According to Adrien Stoutenburg, being a lover of cats (which she is) and a watcher of birds (which she is) "can create a conflict."

A native of Minnesota and now a resident of Lagunitas, California, the author has written over forty books for young people. She won the Academy of American Poets Lamont Award in 1964 for *Heroes, Advise Us,* her first volume of poems. In 1969 she received the California Commonwealth Club's silver medal for the most distinguished book of poems by a California author. It was awarded for her second volume, *Short History of the Fur Trade.*

Sy Katzoff has been a free-lance photographer since 1950. He lives in New York City, where he shares his home with a black, white, and handsome cat called Hypo.

Three of his first books — *Barto Takes the Subway* and *Amy's Doll,* written by Barbara Brenner, and *Kathy's First School,* written by his wife Betty — are especially popular with young readers.

811
Sto

6291

Stoutenburg, Adrien
A Cat Is

Hugh Mercer School